The Secret Garden

Garden of Dreams

———————

Hina Victor

Dedication

To every one of the people who have tracked down comfort, motivation, and the persevering through sorcery of nature in the safe-haven of a secret nursery. May the magnificence of the regular world always contact your hearts and help you to remember the unlimited potential for recharging and change that lives inside every one of us.

This book is devoted to the visionaries, the nursery workers, and the attendants of mystery places, who comprehend that in the calmest corners, the most phenomenal stories and supernatural occurrences can befound.

Hina Victor

Table of Contents

Foreword

In the realm of writing, certain stories have a special charm, their words and subjects rising above existence to spellbind a large number of ages. "The Mystery Nursery" is one such story — an immortal jewel that has held a unique spot in the hearts of perusers for north of a really long period.

Frances Hodgson Burnett's work of art, first distributed in quite a while, an enchanted all its own. It welcomes us to enter an existence where dismissed nurseries can be changed into shelters of excellence, where the human soul can be restored, and where the obligations of fellowship can recuperate even the most profound injuries.

The force of nature, the flexibility of the human heart, and the faith in the unprecedented conceivable outcomes that life holds have made "The Mystery Nursery" a persevering and adored story. Its subjects of reestablishment and change keep on impacting us, offering a brief look into the significant limit of the human soul to defeat misfortune and prosper.

As you venture through the pages of this book, let the charm of the mystery garden divert you. Investigate the secret corners, uncover the secrets, and feel the murmurs of nature contact your spirit. May you track down motivation in the story of Mary, Colin, and the nursery that united them, and may you convey the persevering through message of trust, fellowship, and the endless magnificence of the normal world with you.

Welcome to the universe of "The Mystery Nursery." It is an existence where the customary becomes uncommon, where the neglected is recollected, and where the heart tracks down its direction back to the enchantment of life itself.

Hina Victor

Preface

In the secret corners of the scholarly world, there exist stories that have a novel power — the ability to move us to places we've never been, to uncover mysteries we've never envisioned, and to help us to remember the immortal miracles of the regular world. "The Mystery Nursery" is one such story — an exemplary that has held ages in its bondage, showing us the strength of the human soul and the persevering through excellence of nature.

First wrote by Frances Hodgson Burnett in 1911, "The Mystery Nursery" has been esteemed by perusers, all things considered. Its story is one of change, of stowed away magnificence uncovered, and of the phenomenal capability of the human heart. A story welcomes us to enter an existence where trust and restoration come out from the actual earth, where neglected places become safe-havens of recuperating, and where the obligations of fellowship are fashioned in the most improbable of settings.

In these pages, we set out on an excursion into the core of the story, where a little kid named Mary, a slight kid named Colin, and a long-disregarded garden meet to make an embroidery of sorcery and marvel. As we follow their experiences, we are reminded that even in the most startling spots, we can track down the keys to open our own secret possibilities and the significant limit of the human soul to conquer difficulty and thrive.

Through "The Mystery Nursery," we are acquainted with an existence where nature's excellence is a mirror for the magnificence that dwells inside every one of us, where the demonstration of sustaining life is an extraordinary power, and where the commitment of recharging is ever-present. It is a reality where conventional kids set out on uncommon excursions, and where the demonstration of keeping an eye on a nursery turns into a representation for watching out for one's own heart.

As you turn the pages of this book, permit yourself to be shipped to the captivating universe of the mystery garden. Tune in for the murmurs of nature, let the aromas of sprouting blossoms fill your faculties, and take comfort in the thought that, very much like the nursery, you also have the ability to recuperate, to develop, and to bloom.

The enchantment of "The Mystery Nursery" looks for you, prepared to help you to remember the persevering through excellence and unfathomable potential that live both in the normal world and inside the profundities of your own heart.

Hina Victor

Introduction

Welcome to a reality where nature holds the way in to the exceptional, where the excellence of the normal world conceals mysteries that can mend the human heart and change lives. "The Mystery Nursery" is an immortal exemplary that welcomes you to investigate this world, to reveal its secrets, and to encounter the enchanted that dwells inside its pages.

Frances Hodgson Burnett's adored novel, first distributed in quite a while, enchanted perusers for ages with its getting through topics of trust, flexibility, and the wondrous capability of the human soul. A story rises above time, enamoring the hearts of both youthful and old, and conveying a message that keeps on resounding today.

The excursion starts with Mary Lennox, a little kid who, following a misfortune, ends up under the watchful eye of far off family members at the puzzling Misselthwaite House. There, she finds the privileged insights of the house as well as a long-neglected, stowed away nursery — a captivating space loaded up with congested plants, old roses, and a commitment of restoration.

As Mary's undertakings unfurl, we are acquainted with a cast of characters, each bearing their own injuries and insider facts. Through the nursery, they find a safe-haven for the body as well as a safe-haven for the spirit. The nursery's change reflects their own, a demonstration of the force of nature and the human soul to recuperate and develop.

"The Mystery Nursery" is an account of recovery, of enlivening, and of the conviction that, in the most unforeseen spots, we can track down the keys to open our secret possibilities. It is an account of the excellence of the regular world as an impression of the magnificence that dwells inside every one of us.

In the accompanying pages, you will step into the universe of Mary, Colin, and the mystery garden. You will be shipped to where the customary becomes remarkable, where neglected spaces are stirred, and where the demonstration of keeping an eye on life turns into a groundbreaking power.

The mystery nursery's enchantment isn't restricted to its pages; a world can rouse, recuperate, and help us to remember the endless magnificence that lives inside the profundities of our own hearts. Thus, as you leave on this excursion, permit the nursery's murmurs to contact your spirit and the scent of its blooms to fill your faculties. Let its getting through message of trust and recharging be your directing light.

Welcome to the charming universe of "The Mystery Nursery," where the way to change lies in the least complex of things: the demonstration of keeping an eye on life and the persevering through faith in the remarkable potential that dwells inside every one of us.

Hina Victor

Chapter 1
The Hidden Sanctuary

It was a dim and cloudy morning when Mary Lennox showed up at Misselthwaite House. The carriage shocked to a stop, and the driver opened the entryway, uncovering a rambling, ivy-shrouded chateau encompassed by gardens that had tragically missing their radiance. Mary, a slender, dull confronted young lady with wide, inquisitive eyes, ventured out onto the cobblestone carport, grasping her worn out doll.

"Is this it?" she asked in an exhausted tone, looking over the stupendous yet decrepit house.

The driver gestured and highlighted the overwhelming front entryways. "Yes, Miss. Welcome to Misselthwaite."

Mary's folks had passed on in India, passing on her a vagrant with nobody to really focus on her. She was currently under the guardianship of her uncle, Archibald Timid, who resided in the immense, bleak house with 100 locked entryways.

The maid, Mrs. Medlock, met Mary at the entry and guided her inside. Mary couldn't resist the opportunity to see the harsh, unsmiling attitude of the lady. She rushed to illuminate Mary that she would be let for the most part alone.

"Your uncle doesn't wish to be upset, and he's away more often than not," Mrs. Medlock made sense of.

Mary was directed to her room, a cold and grim chamber with weighty draperies that shut out the light. She really wanted to feel an ache of forlornness as she unloaded her small effects. With her folks gone and her new watchman apathetic, she felt completely alone on the planet.

Days transformed into weeks, and Mary developed increasingly separated. She wandered the lobbies of the estate, investigating its vast passageways and dusty, neglected rooms. One stormy evening, while at the same time looking for cover from the deluge, she coincidentally found a vital swinging from a snare in the corridor.

Interest got the better of her, and she took the critical in, not entirely set in stone to find what it opened. After some looking, she found an entryway that appeared to match the critical's size and shape. With a shaking hand, she turned the critical in the lock and pushed the entryway open.

What lay past was a disclosure. It was a secret nursery, congested and went head to head with weeds, yet at the same time, it held a wild and untamed excellence. Mary panted at seeing it. She had coincidentally found a long-failed to remember safe-haven, stowed away from the world.

As Mary ventured into the nursery, the air was loaded up with the wonderful fragrance of earth and the melodies of concealed birds. She knew at that time that she had uncovered something uncommon. The nursery had turned into her mysterious, her asylum from the forlornness that had wrapped her.

Little did Mary had any idea that this secret safe-haven would completely change herself in manners she would never have envisioned, carrying with it the wizardry of nature as well as the commitment of kinship and change

Chapter 2
In the Heart of the Secret Garden

As the days passed, Mary's mysterious outings to the secret nursery turned into an esteemed everyday practice. She would escape her room, conveying her little planting instruments, and clear her path through the labyrinth of lobbies to the entryway that prompted the nursery. With each visit, the once-dismissed garden changed before her eyes.

Her little, gloved hands worked indefatigably to gather up the tangled weeds, uncovering the failed to remember excellence that lay underneath. There were roses of each and every variety, their petals sensitive and fragrant, and ivy-covered entrances that murmured privileged insights as the breeze stirred through their leaves. Sculptures of holy messengers and creatures enhanced the corners, their endured faces appearing to grin down on Mary.

With each stroke of her spade, Mary felt a feeling of direction she had never experienced. The nursery turned into her comfort, where her depression dissolved away in the organization of blossoming blossoms and the ensemble of nature's sounds.

One morning, as she watched out for the roses, Mary saw a bizarre, green shoot rising up out of the earth. It was not normal for any plant she had seen previously, with flimsy, spindly leaves and a need to get a move on in its development. She chose to research further and delicately cleared the dirt around it.

To her awe, a small entryway was uncovered at the foundation of the plant, no greater than her hand. It was not normal for any entryway she had at any point seen, embellished with mind boggling carvings of departs and blossoms. Fervor flooded through her, and without a second thought, she pushed the entryway open.

As the entryway squeaked open, Mary ended up in a secret chamber underneath the nursery. It was a little, faintly lit space, however what caught her consideration was a picture holding tight the wall. It was a painting of a young lady with kind, brilliant eyes and a brilliant grin. Mary felt an illogical association with the lady in the composition, as though she were checking a tragically missing companion out.

Underneath the representation, a written by hand note read, "To the person who tracks down this nursery, may it give you pleasure and recuperating. — L."

Mary couldn't contain her interest. Who was "L"? What was the story behind this secret chamber? The more she investigated, the more inquiries emerged.

Throughout the next weeks, Mary dove further into the nursery's secrets, revealing the mysteries of the actual nursery as well as the historical backdrop of the people who had adored and watched out for it before. Every disclosure carried her nearer to understanding the genuine enchantment of the secret safe-haven and the significant effect it would have on her life.

In any case, what Mary didn't yet acknowledge was that the nursery held another mystery, one that would change her own fate as well as that of one more desolate soul who longed for the glow of fellowship and the revival of a long-failed to remember heart.

Chapter 3
Blossoms and Mysteries

As the days transformed into weeks, Mary's connection to the mystery garden extended. It was her sanctuary, where the heaviness of her dejection appeared to dissipate as time passes. With each visit, the nursery uncovered a greater amount of its secret fortunes, both as lively blooms and the cryptic secrets that encompassed it.

One radiant morning, Mary set out with a feeling of fervor. She had found a locked entryway at the furthest finish of the nursery, canvassed in plants and covered by a shrubbery of roses. This entryway held the commitment of one more secret corner of the nursery, and not entirely set in stone to uncover its mysteries.

After some work, Mary figured out how to clean up the congested plants and find the key that would open the entryway. As she turned the weighty iron key in the lock, a sensation of expectation washed over her. She pushed the entryway open, uncovering a lavish, immaculate part of the nursery.

This piece of the nursery was not the same as the rest. It was a universe of wild magnificence, with tall, influencing grasses and bunches of wildflowers in shades of purple, gold, and blue. The air was loaded up with the murmur of honey bees and the delicate stirring of leaves in the breeze.

In the focal point of this wild heaven stood an eminent tree, its branches extending wide and its leaves gleaming with a brilliant tint. At its base, a little stone seat welcomed Mary to sit and take in the peaceful environmental factors.

As Mary investigated this new region, she found a secret way that prompted a shining stream, its waters hitting the dance floor with the impression of the daylight. She followed the stream further into the nursery until she happened upon a clearing where the most phenomenal sight looked for her.

There, settled among the tall grasses, was a circle of splendidly hued mushrooms. Each mushroom was an alternate tint, and they appeared to gleam with a powerful light. Mary couldn't fight the temptation to contact one, and as her fingers brushed against the sensitive cap, a delicate, tinkling sound consumed the space.

It was a sound like giggling, and Mary couldn't resist the opportunity to grin. The nursery had a bigger number of mysteries than she had at any point envisioned, and still up in the air to uncover them all.

As she kept on investigating, Mary's heart was loaded up with a feeling of marvel and experience. She felt a profound association with the nursery and a developing craving to gain proficiency with history and the tales of those had cherished it before.

In any case, in the midst of the magnificence and charm, Mary likewise detected a significant pity that appeared to wait in the air. It was a secret that pulled at her heart, and she realize that there was something else to find about the secret safe-haven and the lives it had contacted.

Little did Mary had any idea about that her excursion into the core of the mystery garden was simply starting, and that the blooms and secrets that looked for her wouldn't just change her own life yet additionally the existences of people around her

Chapter 4
Unlocking the Garden's Secrets

Mary's days at Misselthwaite Estate had gone through an exceptional change since the disclosure of the mystery garden. No longer did she feel the smothering load of dejection; all things considered, her heart was loaded up with the expectation of her everyday visits to the secret safe-haven.

Every morning, she would get out of her room and advance toward the nursery, where she would watch out for the blossoms, investigate the winding ways, and search out new secrets that lay tucked away among the leaves and plants.

One bright evening, as she was pruning the roses close to the nursery's edge, Mary saw something curious. She had heard bits of hearsay from the workers about a strange, secured entryway in the estate that prompted a long-neglected piece of the house. She had consistently excused these stories as inactive tattle, yet presently, she really wanted to contemplate whether there was any reality to them.

With newly discovered assurance, Mary chose to examine. She followed her instinct and remembered her means through the nursery to the secret chamber she had found before. It was there that she tracked down an old, iron key holding tight a snare. It was comparable in size and shape to the key she had used to open the nursery's entryway.

With the vital close by, Mary got back to the estate and started her quest for the baffling locked entryway. She investigated the faintly lit passageways and flights of stairs, directed simply by the gleaming light of her flame. At last, she coincidentally found a weighty wooden entryway with a lavish lock that matched the key.

As she turned the vital in the lock and pushed the entryway open, Mary felt a surge of fervor. She had opened another secret, one that prompted the core of Misselthwaite House itself.

Inside, she found a room loaded up with dusty old books, blurred embroideries, and failed to remember relics of the past. The room had a long-deserted feel, as though it had been immaculate for a really long time. Yet, what really caught Mary's consideration was an enormous, luxurious mirror that held tight the far wall.

The mirror was not normal for any she had at any point seen. Its casing was enhanced with perplexing carvings of blossoms and plants, and its surface sparkled with a supernatural light. Mary couldn't avoid moving toward it, her appearance faltering as she moved nearer.

As she looked into the mirror, Mary felt a weird sensation, as though the mirror held the ability to uncover stowed away insights. She watched in wonder as the reflection before her started to move and change, showing scenes from an earlier time.

She saw a young lady with long, streaming hair keeping an eye on the nursery, her giggling consuming the space. She saw youngsters playing among the roses, their countenances overflowing with delight. She saw the nursery in its full brilliance, a position of excellence and satisfaction.

Maybe the mirror were showing her the historical backdrop of the nursery, the narratives of the people who had adored it and supported it. Mary was enraptured by the scenes unfurling before her, and she realize that she had opened a mother lode of privileged insights that would carry her nearer to understanding the nursery's actual enchantment.

As Mary kept on investigating the room, she found diaries and letters that had a place with the past occupants of the estate. She found out about a lady named Lily, who had made the nursery and emptied her heart into its excellence. She found that Lily had abandoned a tradition of adoration and satisfaction, an inheritance that Mary presently felt a sense of urgency to convey forward.

With freshly discovered reason, Mary made plans to reestablish the nursery to its previous magnificence and to reveal the narratives of the people who had valued it before. She realize that the nursery held the way to opening not exclusively its own insider facts yet in addition the mysteries of her own heart.

As she ventured once more into the nursery, the sun plunged underneath the skyline, projecting a warm, brilliant sparkle over the blossoms and trees. Mary felt a significant feeling of appreciation for the nursery and the secrets it had uncovered to her. She realize that her process was not even close to finished, and she was anxious to keep investigating the secret profundities of the nursery's wizardry.

Chapter 5
The Enchanted Garden Chronicles

As Mary kept on digging into the secrets of the secret nursery, she likewise left on a journey to become familiar with individuals who had cherished and watched out for it before. She had tracked down diaries and letters in the mystery chamber, and each piece of composing uncovered another layer of the nursery's set of experiences.

One night, while perusing the diaries, Mary ran over a passage that provoked her interest. It discussed a secret diary, a journal that had a place with Lily, the one who had made the nursery. This journal was said to contain the most close subtleties of Lily's life and her profound association with the nursery.

Not entirely set in stone to find this lacking part of the riddle, Mary set off on a mission to look through the estate again. She investigated the secret corners and dusty upper rooms, investigating every possibility. It was during one of these hunts that she coincidentally found a little, failed to remember library concealed on the highest level.

The library was a gold mine of old books, guides, and reports. Among the racks, Mary found an old cowhide bound diary with the name "Lily" emblazoned in gold letters on the cover. Her heart dashed with fervor as she opened the pages and started to peruse.

In the journal, Lily's words showed signs of life. She expounded on her profound love for the nursery, her fantasies about making a position of excellence and shelter, and her assurance to resurrect the nursery. Mary felt a significant association with the lady whose words filled the pages, as though Lily's soul lived on in the actual nursery.

As Mary kept on perusing, she found out about Lily's battles and wins, her snapshots of uncertainty and her resolute assurance. Lily had confronted her own difficulties, similarly as Mary endlessly had tracked down comfort and reason in the nursery.

In any case, there was something else to the journal besides Lily's own appearance. Mary likewise found traces of a secret fortune, a mysterious that had been gone down through the ages. It was supposed to be a key that would open the nursery's most prominent wizardry.

With newly discovered assurance, Mary left on a journey to track down this secret fortune and to uncover the genuine influence of the nursery. She followed the pieces of information abandoned by Lily, signs that drove her more profound into the core of the nursery and to the very place where the fortune was supposed to be covered up.

One brilliant morning, as the sun sifted through the leaves and the birds sang their tunes, Mary ended up remaining before a little, genuine stone platform. On top of the platform, she found a brilliant key, its unpredictable plan mirroring the magnificence of the actual nursery.

As Mary got the key, a feeling of expectation consumed the space. She realize that she grasped the way to opening the nursery's most noteworthy insider facts, to uncovering the full degree of its charm.

In any case, as she remained there, key close by, Mary likewise understood that the genuine wizardry of the nursery was not simply in its secret fortunes or its secrets. It was in the association she had produced with the nursery, in the kinships she had framed, and in the change that had occurred inside her own heart.

With a profound feeling of appreciation and a reestablished feeling of direction, Mary made a guarantee to the nursery and to herself. She would keep on investigating its captivating profundities, to reveal its privileged insights, and to convey forward the tradition of affection and magnificence that Lily had made.

Also, as she ventured into the core of the nursery, key close by, Mary realize that the undertakings of the secret safe-haven were nowhere near finished. The charmed nursery had a lot more stories to tell, and she was anxious to turn into a piece of its persevering through narratives.

Chapter 6
A Garden's Whispers

With the brilliant key in her control, Mary felt a feeling of expectation and miracle that appeared to saturate each edge of the nursery. She knew that the critical held the ability to open the nursery's most prominent insider facts, yet she additionally comprehended that those mysteries were not to be disentangled quickly.

As Mary proceeded with her everyday visits to the nursery, she saw unpretentious changes in its environment. The air appeared to murmur with another energy, and the blossoms seemed to sprout with much more prominent liveliness. Maybe the actual nursery was getting ready for the uncovering of its secrets.

One night, as the sun plunged beneath the skyline and the nursery was washed in the delicate gleam of dusk, Mary concluded the time had come to utilize the brilliant key. She advanced toward the core of the nursery, where the platform had stood, and she embedded the key into a secret lock inside the stone.

With a delicate turn of the key, a delicate snap reverberated through the nursery, and a pathway showed up before her. It was a way she had never seen, driving further into the core of the nursery. As Mary ventured onto the way, she felt a feeling of veneration and expectation, like she were entering a hallowed domain.

The way wound its direction through a shelter of blooming trees and fragile blossoms, each step loaded up with the murmurs of nature. Birds sang sweet tunes above, and the scent of sprouting roses swirled around. Mary followed the way with a feeling of miracle, directed by the charming magnificence that encompassed her.

As she strolled, Mary saw that the way was fixed with little, gleaming circles. They appeared to drift in mid-air, projecting a delicate, ethereal light. Each circle radiated a mitigating, melodic murmur that resounded with the musicality of the nursery.

The way in the end drove Mary to a peaceful, twilight clearing. In the focal point of the clearing stood a grand tree, its branches extending high into the night sky. Underneath the tree, a roundabout stone platform held a book bound in sparkling, emerald leaves.

Mary moved toward the book with a combination of worship and interest. It was not normal for any book she had at any point seen, its pages made of sensitive petals that appeared to vacillate with each breath of wind. She connected and opened the book, uncovering pages loaded up with words that appeared to move and change, as though they were alive.

The words on the pages recounted the account of the nursery, from its creation by Lily to the snapshots of euphoria and distress that had unfurled inside its walls. They discussed the nursery's sorcery, its ability to recuperate and change, and the profound association it shaped with the people who really focused on it.

However, the book likewise uncovered something more significant — a message that appeared to reverberate profound inside Mary's heart. It discussed the significance of adoration, kinship, and the excellence that could be tracked down even in the most surprising spots. It reminded Mary that the genuine wizardry of the nursery was not in its mysteries but rather in the association it encouraged and the adoration it propelled.

With tears of appreciation in her eyes, Mary shut the book and felt a profound feeling of satisfaction. She realize that the nursery had given her a gift far more noteworthy than any fortune or secret. It had provided her a feeling of motivation, a local area of companions, and where her heart could genuinely bloom.

As she advanced back along the way, Mary understood that the nursery's murmurs were the privileged insights it held as well as the delicate tokens of the magnificence and miracle that encompassed her consistently. What's more, that's what she knew, as long as she watched out for the nursery with affection and care, its sorcery would keep on prospering, rousing all who entered its charming domain.

Chapter 7
Garden of Dreams

As the days transformed into weeks, Mary kept on investigating the captivating profundities of the mystery garden. The nursery had turned into a position of comfort, a material for her fantasies, and a safe-haven where she felt genuinely alive. However, Mary had likewise come to understand that the nursery held a considerably more prominent reason — a reason that went past its excellence and secrets.

One bright morning, Mary chose to welcome Colin, her cousin and the beneficiary of Misselthwaite House, to the nursery. Colin had consumed a large portion of his time on earth restricted to his room because of a disease that had left him powerless and disabled. He had never encountered the wizardry of the nursery, and Mary accepted that it could hold the way in to his recuperating.

With a feeling of expectation, Mary advanced toward Colin's room and found him sitting by the window, pale and slight. She made sense of the miracles of the mystery garden, the magnificence of the blossoms, and the recuperating power that appeared to exude from its actual soil. Colin, at first doubtful, consented to go with her to the nursery.

As they entered the nursery together, Colin's eyes enlarged in wonder. The dynamic tones, the fragrant blooms, and the delicate breeze that stirred through the leaves filled him with a feeling of marvel he had never known. Maybe the nursery had become fully awake to invite him.

Mary directed Colin to the core of the nursery, where the flickering book of emerald leaves lay upon the stone platform. She

urged him to open the book and read the expressions of the nursery
— the tales of adoration, recuperating, and change.

As Colin read, a feeling of trust and essentialness flooded
through him. Maybe the nursery's sorcery was reinvigorating his
debilitated body. He shut his eyes, and without precedent for
years, he experienced the glow of the sun all over and the earth
underneath his feet.

With Mary's help, Colin started to investigate the nursery, his
means developing further as time passes. He watched out for the
blossoms, paid attention to the melodies of the birds, and permitted
the charm of the nursery to implant his soul. The additional time
he spent in the nursery, the more he felt its mending power
flowing through him.

In any case, it wasn't simply the actual recuperating that the
nursery offered; it was likewise a mending of the substance.
Colin's once-reserved disposition started to relax, and he framed a
profound association with Mary, who had turned into his closest
companion.

As the seasons changed and the nursery blossomed with new
life, Mary and Colin's bond developed further. They shared their
fantasies, their feelings of trepidation, and their expectations for
what's to come. They accepted that the nursery held the ability to
mend their bodies as well as their spirits, and still up in the air to
capitalize on each second they spent inside its charmed hug.

The nursery had turned into a position of dreams, where the
inconceivable appeared to be conceivable, and where love and
fellowship could genuinely bloom. It was a demonstration of the
persevering through force of nature, the flexibility of the human
soul, and the enchanted that could be tracked down in the most
unforeseen spots.

Thus, as Mary and Colin kept on investigating the nursery of dreams, they realize that its charm would stay with them, directing them on their excursion of recuperating, change, and the endless potential outcomes that lay ahead.

Chapter 8
The Secret Garden Reimagined

As time passes, the enchantment of the mystery garden kept on winding around its spell over Mary, Colin, and the whole family of Misselthwaite House. The nursery had turned into a position of recuperating, change, and solid obligations of kinship. Its accounts of adoration and recharging had contacted the hearts of the people who entered its charming domain.

As the nursery prospered under Mary and Colin's consideration, its excellence started to spread past the nursery walls. The roses that whenever had been dismissed now blossomed with energetic varieties that appeared to light the very air with their scent. The ivy-shrouded passages turned into an image of the nursery's getting through strength, and the sculptures of holy messengers and creatures appeared to show some signs of life in the dappled daylight.

Insight about the nursery's change arrived at the workers, the residents, and, surprisingly, the antisocial uncle, Archibald Fainthearted, who had been missing for quite a bit of Mary and Colin's experiences. He got back to Misselthwaite House, drawn by the murmurs of the nursery's resurrection.

At the point when he saw the nursery in the entirety of its radiant greatness, he was overwhelmed with feeling. The nursery, which had once been a position of distress and disregard, had been changed into a living embroidery of magnificence and trust. Maybe the soul of his late spouse, Lily, had gotten back to him through the nursery she had loved.

Archibald Timid joined Mary, Colin, and the workers in the nursery, and without precedent for years, he experienced the glow of the sun all over and the earth underneath his feet. It was a snapshot of compromise, a get-together of a family that had been broken by misery and misfortune.

The nursery had not just mended the assortments of Mary and Colin however had likewise recuperated the injuries of their souls. It had united individuals from various different backgrounds, joining them in their adoration for the nursery and their common encounters of development and change.

As the years passed, the nursery's wizardry kept on flourishing. Mary and Colin developed further and dynamic people, their bond with one another and the nursery more grounded than at any other time. The nursery turned into a position of comfort and motivation, a wellspring of vast stories and undertakings.

To pay tribute to Lily's memory and the inheritance she had abandoned, the nursery was reconsidered as a position of local area and inventiveness. It turned into a safe-haven for the Fearful family as well as for the residents of the encompassing open country. They accumulated in the nursery to share their fantasies, make craftsmanship, and commend the magnificence of nature.

The nursery of Misselthwaite Estate turned into an image of reestablishment and change, a demonstration of the getting through force of affection, companionship, and the enchantment of the regular world. Its charm was not restricted to its walls however transmitted out into the existences of all who embraced its insider facts and its excellence.

Thus, the narrative of "The Secret Safe-haven" was as of now not simply a story of a dismissed nursery and the forlorn spirits who had found its sorcery. It was an account of a nursery rethought, where dreams were understood, and where the murmurs of nature and the human heart interweaved to make a heritage that would persevere for a long time into the future.

Chapter 9
Garden of Healing

The nursery of Misselthwaite Estate had turned into an encouraging sign and change, where the obligations of kinship had developed further, and where dreams took off on the wings of creative mind. It had contacted the existences of all who entered its charming hug, carrying recuperating and recharging to every one.

Mary, Colin, and Archibald Fainthearted kept on spending their days in the nursery, keeping an eye on its lavish sprouts and paying attention to the narratives murmured by the stirring leaves. The nursery had turned into a safe-haven for them, where they could abandon the scars of their past and embrace the commitment of a more promising time to come.

Colin, when laid up and fragile, had developed into a powerful and lively young fellow. The nursery had made all the difference for his wellbeing, yet it had likewise supported his soul. He had found a profound love for nature and an energy for organic science, and he longed for one day turning into a famous horticulturist.

Mary had tracked down her bringing in the nursery also. She had a characteristic ability for cajoling life from the dirt, and her green thumb had transformed the nursery into a work of art of variety and scent. She had additionally turned into a supporter for the recuperating force of nurseries, imparting her insight and enthusiasm to the residents and in any event, visiting emergency clinics to give the pleasure of cultivating to those out of luck.

Archibald Cowardly had come to treasure the nursery as an association with his late spouse, Lily. He went through hours strolling among the roses and paying attention to the tunes of the birds, tracking down comfort and a feeling of conclusion in the nursery's magnificence. It was where he felt Lily's presence most intensely, where he could recollect their affection and the existence they had once shared.

The nursery had likewise turned into a position of festivity and local area. The locals of the encompassing wide open assembled routinely to share their accounts, make workmanship, and revel in the normal magnificence that encompassed them. The nursery had united individuals, crossing over the holes that had once partitioned them.

In any case, maybe the most noteworthy change was the impact the nursery had on the whole family of Misselthwaite Estate. The workers, who had once approached their obligations with a feeling of separation, presently tracked down comfort and motivation in the nursery's excellence. They, as well, had found their own secret gifts and interests, whether it was painting, singing, or essentially tracking down euphoria in the straightforward demonstration of watching out for the blossoms.

As the years passed, the nursery kept on prospering, its sorcery undiminished. It had turned into an image of recuperating, a demonstration of the flexibility of the human soul, and an update that even the most disregarded spots could be changed into sanctuaries of magnificence and restoration.

The tale of the mystery garden had risen above its unique account. It was at this point not a story of a forlorn young lady and a dismissed nursery however an account of recovery, development, and the getting through force of adoration and fellowship. The nursery had turned into a living demonstration of the conviction that, with care and supporting, even the most broken hearts and spirits could track down recuperating and reestablishment.

Chapter 10
Lost and Found in the Secret Garden

As the years moved on, the mystery nursery of Misselthwaite Estate stayed a position of magnificence, marvel, and mending. The nursery had woven its charm not just into the existences of Mary, Colin, and Archibald Cowardly yet in addition into the hearts of all who had been moved by its enchantment.

Mary and Colin had developed into certain and humane people, their adoration for one another and the nursery extending as time passes. They had satisfied their fantasies and had become stewards of the nursery's heritage, imparting stories and insider facts to those looked for its comfort.

Archibald Timid, as well, experienced tracked down a proportion of harmony in the nursery's hug. He had dealt with his melancholy and had tracked down solace in the recollections of his better half, Lily. The nursery had turned into a position of reflection and restoration, a living recognition for the love they had shared.

In any case, the nursery held one last confidential, a mysterious that would contact the existences of all who had been a piece of its story. It was a mysterious that had been murmured by the actual nursery, a mysterious that had been ready to be found.

One fresh pre-winter morning, as Mary and Colin walked around the nursery, they saw a little, honest entryway tucked away among the ivy-shrouded passages. It was an entryway they had never seen, and it appeared to coax to them with a feeling of secret.

With interest in their souls, they moved toward the entryway and found that it prompted a secret chamber underneath the nursery, similar as the one Mary had found quite a while back. In any case, this chamber was unique — it was loaded up with ancient rarities and tokens from Lily's life.

As Mary and Colin investigated the chamber, they uncovered letters, representations, and mementos that uncovered the profundity of Lily's association with the nursery. They found out about her fantasies and yearnings, her affection for the normal world, and her craving to make a position of excellence and mending.

However, what bewildered them more than anything was a letter that discussed a secret fortune — a fortune that Lily had shared with the nursery's consideration. It was a fortune that had the influence to change lives and to get desire to those need.

Sincerely and fervor, Mary and Colin followed the hints left by Lily, setting out on a mission to track down the secret fortune. They looked through the nursery, unraveling conundrums and following a path of blossoming blossoms and sparkling spheres.

At last, in a confined corner of the nursery, they revealed the fortune — a little, brilliant key, similar as the one that had opened the actual nursery. It was a critical that held the ability to make a way for a fresh start, an entryway that would prompt a more promising time to come.

As Mary and Colin grasped the key, they realize that it was an image of the nursery's getting through sorcery and the adoration that had united them. It was an update that, even in the haziest of times, there was dependably a key to open the way to trust and change.

With the vital close by, Mary and Colin advanced toward the core of the nursery, where another entryway had showed up, washed in a delicate, brilliant light. They opened the entryway together, their hearts loaded up with expectation and appreciation.

On the opposite side of the entryway, they tracked down a stunning sight — a nursery significantly more lovely and charming than the one they had known. It was a nursery of dreams, where wishes materialized and where the wizardry of the heart could make supernatural occurrences.

As Mary and Colin ventured into the nursery of dreams, they realize that their process was not even close to finished. The nursery had uncovered its last confidential, confidential of limitless conceivable outcomes and the force of adoration to change lives.

Thus, in the nursery of dreams, Mary, Colin, and all who had been a piece of its story ended up lost and tracked down in a universe of miracle and charm. It was an existence where the past and what was in store converged into an embroidery of trust, where the magnificence of the normal world and the versatility of the human soul met up as a beautiful, unified whole.

As they strolled inseparably through the nursery of dreams, Mary and Colin realize that their lives had been perpetually changed by the wizardry of the mystery garden. It was an enchanted that had recuperated their bodies, patched their hearts, and shown them the boundless capability of the human soul.

What's more, as the nursery murmured its last mysteries to the breeze, it conveyed with it a message of trust and reestablishment, a message that would live on in the hearts of all who had been moved by its charm.